Abortion Road Trip

A full-length play by Rachel Lynett

Uproar Theatrics

LICENSING & PRODUCTION INQUIRIES
Uproar Theatrics, LLC.
hello@uproartheatrics.com I www.UproarTheatrics.com

CHARACTERS
LEXA, 25, not white MINNIE, 28, not white

DRIVER, early thirties, white

QUINN, late twenties, MINNIE's girlfriend, any race

MOM, Lexa and Minnie's mom, early thirties a different race from LEXA and MINNIE TAYLOR**, DRIVER's partner, early thirties, any race
(* In the play, Mom only appears in the past when she would've been about thirty two) (**Taylor and Quinn can be played by the same actress but it must be clear that they are different people)

SETTINGS
2016. The play takes place in a taxi cab. They are traveling from Houston, TX to Albuquerque, NM. The space is not literal and the characters step out and even run into their memories.

PRODUCTION HISTORY
Abortion Road Trip premiered at the 2017 DC Capital Fringe Festival. It was presented by Theatre Prometheus (DC). A special production of Abortion Road Trip was featured as part of the Kennedy Center's 2017 Page to Stage Festival, presented by Theatre Prometheus.

ACT 1

LEXA, MINNIE, and DRIVER are all in a taxi cab. LEXA fidgets nervously. MINNIE searches aggressively through her bag. DRIVER tries not to notice.

MINNIE

Can I smoke in here?

LEXA shoots MINNIE a look.

DRIVER

I'd rather you didn't.

MINNIE lights her cigarette.

LEXA

She asked you not to.

MINNIE

I'm stressed out.

LEXA

Why are you stressed out?

MINNIE

This is a stressful situation.

LEXA

It's not your situation.

MINNIE

Then why am I here?

Pause.

DRIVER

I'll just roll the window down.

MINNIE

Thank you.

LEXA

So thanks for taking us all this way.

DRIVER

No problem.

LEXA

My friend Adam said you took him to Dallas once and were cool about it so...

DRIVER

Yeah.

MINNIE

Yeah but New Mexico is like forever away.

LEXA shoots MINNIE a look. MINNIE shrugs.

LEXA

And for being so cool about the price. One driver literally hung up on us.

MINNIE

At the time we were only offering like a grand though. For a twenty four hour trip.

Silence. They were really just talking to fill in the silence.

QUINN comes out on stage outside of the cab.

DRIVER

So what's in New Mexico?

QUINN

Dammit!

LEXA

The end of my life.

DRIVER

Oh.

> *In a separate space, Quinn's locked out of her
> dorm room. She pulls out a book and starts
> reading (it's Nick Flynn).*

> *Only LEXA sees her.*

MINNIE

Seriously Lexa? It's not the end of your life. You're going to
freak her out.

LEXA

I'm going to New Mexico to commit murder.

MINNIE

Jesus.

> *LEXA moves out of the cab and steps into the
> memory . QUINN doesn't look up to see LEXA at
> first. LEXA thinks about walking past but...*

LEXA

Do you need help?

QUINN

Already called the RA.

LEXA

Jennifer?

QUINN nods.

LEXA

It's Saturday night.

QUINN

And?

LEXA

And Jennifer parties every Saturday. Hard. Are you locked out?

QUINN

I am.

LEXA

I could...break in for you.

QUINN stares at LEXA.

LEXA

Okay, okay. Don't look at me like that. If you want to get into your room tonight and not deal with Drunk Jen, you might as well let me try.

QUINN

What's to stop you from breaking into my room another night?

LEXA

Basic human decency.

QUINN continues to stare at LEXA.

4

LEXA

So Nick Flynn huh? That's

QUINN

It's not as pretentious when you're actually from Boston.
And I'm

LEXA

I wasn't going to say

QUINN

You were. And alright. Fine.

LEXA

Alright?

QUINN

Break into my room. I've got a paper on literature of the
homeless I need to finish.

LEXA

Oh. That why you're reading...

QUINN

That's why.

LEXA

I'm sorry I called you pretentious.

QUINN

You didn't. I did. I'm Quinn.

LEXA

Lexa. And to be fair, that's one of my favorite books. I'm
just deeply ashamed about it.

As LEXA is about to "break into" Quinn's room, her phone makes a sound.

MINNIE
(from in the cab)
Could you please put your phone on silent?

LEXA walks back into the cab and out of the memory. DRIVER sits uncomfortably.

LEXA
No. That'll just freak him out.

MINNIE
How would he even know?

LEXA
Because I wouldn't respond.

MINNIE
You're not responding now.

LEXA pulls out her phone and reads the text. She puts the phone back in her pocket.

LEXA
Shit.

MINNIE
What?

LEXA
He said he loved me. That's it. "I love you."

MINNIE
O-kay. Why is that cause for panic?

LEXA

He always puts "Love ya" or "You da best." He's never
actually said I love you. Not even in person.

MINNIE

You've been with him for how long and he still hasn't said I
love you.

LEXA

Four years. And no. In person he just says "you're my
favorite" which I actually always kind of thought was sweet.
But "I love you." That's heavy. He knows.

MINNIE

He does not know. Give me your phone.

> *LEXA hands over her phone. MINNIE scrolls
> through.*

MINNIE

See. Look. Here. I love you. Three days ago.

LEXA

No. That's I and then a picture of a heart and then you.
That's not I love you.

MINNIE

It's the same thing.

LEXA

It isn't. And you know it. Wouldn't you be suspicious if
Quinn suddenly said I love you after not saying it for years?

MINNIE

There's no way I'd date someone for four years and not
make them say I love you.

LEXA

You can't make a person say I love you.

MINNIE

You can. It goes like this. Do you love me, yes or no? If they say no, it's done-zies. We're through. If they say yes, I say, "I need to hear you say it." And then bam. I love you.

LEXA   (to DRIVER)

Have you ever made someone say I love you to your face?

DRIVER

No.

LEXA

That's weird right?

DRIVER

I don't know that it's weird. I just don't really say I love you to a lot of people.

Pause.

LEXA

He knows.

MINNIE

He does not know.

LEXA

How do I even respond?

MINNIE

Just say it back.

LEXA

I can't.

MINNIE

Why not?

LEXA

It's not true.

MINNIE

Suddenly you don't love him.

LEXA

I don't love him today. I don't love anyone today.

MINNIE

Because of the murder?

LEXA

Yes.

MINNIE

It's not murder.

LEXA

That's not what we learned in Catholic school.

MINNIE

Well calling it murder isn't good for your psyche.

LEXA

My psyche? It's murder. Whatever. I'm fine with it.

MINNIE

You can't take a life that doesn't exist.

LEXA

I can take whatever I want.

MINNIE

Well I'm not comfortable with you calling it murder.

LEXA

This isn't about you. This is about me and Alexis.

MINNIE

Who is Alexis?

LEXA

That's what I'd name my kid. If I were to have it. Have her? Him? How do I do

MINNIE

You can't name a fetus.

LEXA

I can do whatever I want to do. I'm an American.

MINNIE smiles. DRIVER is still uncomfortable.

MINNIE

Remind me why we didn't just fly. It would've been cheaper.

LEXA

I wanted the time to think.

MINNIE

You could think on a plane.

LEXA

All I think about on planes is how angry I am about the tiny seats. And fake air. And mean flight attendants. And

MINNIE

We get it.

MINNIE finishes her cigarette and stares out the window.

Silence. MOM comes out on stage. She is pacing. MINNIE notices. MINNIE doesn't move immediately. MOM steps on something.

MOM

Crap!

MINNIE doesn't move. MOM limps over to the nearest seat and inspects her foot.

MOM
I always do this. Lexa and I got the clumsy gene. You lucked out.

MINNIE leaves the cab and steps into the memory.

MOM
I can't take off work. Does she even want me there?

MINNIE shrugs.

MOM
Are you going to tell her about--

MINNIE

Mom.

MOM
She needs you right now, Min. I know you two aren't...telling her could help her get through this.

MINNIE

If I tell her, then it's real. It's too real. I'm not ready for that yet.

> *MINNIE runs out of the memory and back into the cab. She reaches for her phone and starts texting.*

MOM

I think it could be cathartic. Plus only you know what gas stations have the blue pack of Spirits.

> *MINNIE, still in the cab, ignores her. MOM limps off stage.*

DRIVER

So. Do you know anyone in New Mexico?

> *LEXA shakes her head.*

LEXA

No. My nurse in Houston said I had to go to San Antonio. So my friend, Quinn, takes me to that one and the woman there told me a ton of facts that she's apparently legally required to tell me. But when I say facts, I mean nonsense. Because, like I don't even have any kind of medical knowledge, and most of that sounded like bullshit. And they made me watch this video. It was weird. So I looked it up on my own at home and found that my best bet in New Mexico.

DRIVER

Oh.

LEXA

Yeah! Our mom's best friend died, she fucking died, trying to do an at home abortion. Like what the fuck, Texas? What if a woman can't afford the drive? Am I supposed to just die?

DRIVER nods uncomfortably.

MINNIE
You're going to make her pull over. Can we talk about
something else?

> *LEXA nods and pulls out a piece of paper from
> her pocket.*

LEXA
I wrote an obituary.

MINNIE
Oh for fuck's sake. Please tell me you did not.

LEXA
I totally did. And I'd like to read it.

MINNIE
Now? You want to read it now?

DRIVER
(under her breath)
Please don't read it now.

LEXA
Yes.

MINNIE
Dude no. I am not listening to an obituary you wrote for a
kid who doesn't fucking exist. And will never exist. I will go
on your weird cab drive with you and I will--

LEXA
(reading from the piece of paper)
Alexis Aubrey Pearson was one of the brightest stars to ever shine through--

MINNIE
No dude. No.

LEXA
Through Alexa Marina Pearson's vagina.

MINNIE
Oh my God.

LEXA
Had Alexis been born, he but hopefully she would have been a tennis player in his or preferably her younger years and then grew up to be a politician.

MINNIE
Just say she

LEXA
After somehow surprising everyone with her mad policy making (looking up) Mad as in the slang term. I figure that one's going to stay around forever

MINNIE
I'm sure they'd edit out the slang.

LEXA goes back to reading.

LEXA
with her mad policy making, she first became a city councilman.

                    MINNIE
Lexa

                    LEXA
From there she rose up to mayor. And then governor. And
then she became the first female president of the United
States.

                    MINNIE
Hillary.

                    LEXA
Too soon.

                    MINNIE
Will you stop reading now?

          *LEXA folds up the piece of paper and puts it in
          her pocket. Pause.*

                    LEXA
I'm nervous.

                    MINNIE
I know.

          LEXA   (to DRIVER)
Do you know anyone who had an abortion?

                    DRIVER
Um...

                    MINNIE
You cannot ask that.

LEXA

Why not? It's not like I'm asking if she knew a rapist. Or a serial killer.

MINNIE

You just called abortion murder like two minutes ago.

LEXA   (to DRIVER)

I was kidding. Mostly. About that. I'm like super pro-choice.

Pause.

LEXA   (to DRIVER)

Are you dating anyone?

DRIVER nods.

MINNIE

(under her breath)
Stop asking personal questions, Lexa.

LEXA

(overly dramatic)
Stop calling abortion murder. Stop asking personal questions. What am I supposed to do? Sit and chain smoke like you are?

MINNIE

Read a book or something.

LEXA

You know I nervous talk.

MINNIE

I also know you tend to get too personal too fast with strangers.

LEXA

(ignoring MINNIE)
What's your special person's name?

DRIVER

Taylor.

Taylor comes on stage.

MINNIE

Ambiguous gender. I like it.

DRIVER

She's my wife.

LEXA

So much for ambiguity. How did you two meet? Did you
meet in this cab?

> *DRIVER shakes her head and moves from her
> seat. It should be clear that she is still driving
> and this moment with Taylor occurs in another
> reality.*

DRIVER

(as if seeing Taylor for the first time)
We met at a bar.

TAYLOR approaches DRIVER.

TAYLOR

I should be clear with you. I am a lesbian and I will hit on
you.

DRIVER

Shit.

                         TAYLOR
What?

                         DRIVER
You stole my pick up line.

          TAYLOR smiles and extends her hand.

                         TAYLOR
Taylor.

                         DRIVER
Hi. I'm Kate.

          They shake hands.

                         TAYLOR
Drink?

                         DRIVER
Always.

          *TAYLOR goes to "order a drink" and exits the
          stage. DRIVER returns to her seat.*

                         DRIVER
It was a lesbian bar but there were a ton of straight girls
there. I think Taylor and I were the only lesbians there.

                         MINNIE
That keeps happening. I went to a bar with Quinn that was
supposed to be mostly lesbians. And it was full of straight
girls who, quote "didn't want to get hit on." Like seriously
dude you came to a lesbian bar so no one would hit on you?
You didn't think that through.

          DRIVER nods.

DRIVER

Yup. I guess they assume women hit on women less
aggressively. I don't know.

MINNIE

That's bullshit. That's like patriarchal level bull--

LEXA

If I don't get to rant, neither do you.

MINNIE

Fine.

LEXA

And it's not patriarchal. It's true. As the token straight girl in
this cab, I would rather be hit on by a woman than a man.
You turn down a woman, she leaves you alone. You turn
down a man, he tries to murder you. Like seriously. You can
Google it. Rejected man kills woman. There are thousands of
results.

MINNIE (joking)

But not all men.

DRIVER

Murder seems to be a common theme today.

MINNIE

New topic please.

LEXA

I think if I could talk to a genie right now, I'd wish to go
forward in time. But like hundreds of years in time. Like
3030.

MINNIE

This is your new topic?

LEXA

I also want to punch the inventor of the bra in the face. So I guess I would ask the genie to introduce me to the Doctor.

MINNIE

The Doctor?

LEXA

From Doctor Who.

MINNIE

I thought his name was Doctor Who.

LEXA

Now you're just trying to piss me off.

> *DRIVER laughs and gets slightly more comfortable. QUINN comes out on stage reading All About Love by bell hooks. She is obviously waiting for someone. MINNIE notices but doesn't budge.*

LEXA   (to DRIVER)

What inventor would you want to punch in the face?

DRIVER

Edison.

MINNIE

Wasn't he like the worst?

> *QUINN clears her throat, turns the page, waiting.*

DRIVER

He was.

LEXA

I wonder if Edison would vote in favor of getting rid of abortion clinics.

LEXA stares out. QUINN continues to read. A moment. MINNIE walks over to QUINN.

MINNIE

You know, I really should've seen this coming.

QUINN looks up confused.

QUINN

Okay.

MINNIE

I'm Minnie. Quinn right?

QUINN nods.

MINNIE

Lexa is setting us up. She's not coming.

QUINN closes her book.

QUINN

You're Minnie? As in the Minnie who doesn't even live in Texas?

MINNIE

I just moved back.

QUINN

You look nothing like her.

MINNIE

Yeah. Listen. Could you text Lexa for me? My phone is
dead. Tell her I saw, I was uninterested, I am going home.

QUINN

Uninterested?

MINNIE

Who reads bell hooks in a coffee shop?

QUINN

Why are you and your sister so judgy about what other
people are reading?

MINNIE

Seriously. bell hooks? Is she just the distraction to your
texting?

QUINN

My texting?

MINNIE

Just text her okay. I gotta see if mom can pick me up.

QUINN

I have a girlfriend.

MINNIE

Lexa hates your girlfriend.

MINNIE starts to leave.

QUINN

I borrowed it from Lexa. And yes I am actually reading it.

MINNIE stops.

MINNIE

I'm not like her. I don't...I know it's like super dangerous to
say this but I don't really read for fun. I get bored and I end
up doing something else. So if you really are reading bell
hooks in the middle of the day at a coffee shop this isn't
going to work.

QUINN

How'd she get you here? Like how did she get you to come?

MINNIE

She said she wanted to buy me congrats coffee for
graduating a semester early.

> *QUINN kicks out the chair for MINNIE to sit
> down.*

QUINN

Huh. She told me she was introducing me to her asshole
sister. Because my girlfriend really is the worst.

> *MINNIE smiles. She takes a minute, steps out of
> the memory and back into the cab.*

> *Out of nowhere and suddenly*

MINNIE

I think I want to punch Jefferson in the face.

LEXA

What?

MINNIE

You asked who I'd punch in the face.

                              LEXA
Yeah. A while ago. And like, Thomas Jefferson or Jefferson
that teacher you dated in high school?

                             MINNIE
Oooh. I forgot about him. Both. Definitely both.

                             DRIVER
Why Thomas Jefferson?

                             MINNIE
Why not?

              DRIVER nods. MINNE's phone vibrates.

                             MINNIE
Quinn wants to know if you shaved.

            LEXA looks over at the phone and then laughs.

                              LEXA
I thought you were kidding.

                             MINNIE
Nope. That is an actual text. "Did Lex make sure to shave
her bushy ass vagina?"

                              LEXA
I don't shave for my partners. I'm not shaving for a doctor.

              *MINNIE nods, sends a quick text, and then puts
              her phone away. Pause. LEXA touches her
              stomach.*

                              LEXA
I'd be a shitty mom.

MINNIE

You're 25. Who's a good mom at 25?

LEXA

Our mom was a good mom. And she had you at eighteen.

MINNIE

Our mom was born to be someone's mom. You're holding yourself to an un-achievable standard.

LEXA

Did you have a good mom?

DRIVER

No. Not really .

MINNIE

I don't think mom is happy. Like she's a good mom but she's not happy.

LEXA

Who has a happy mom? Motherhood sucks.

DRIVER laughs at this.

DRIVER

My mom was happy. That's probably why she was shitty.

MINNIE

That's the trade off.

LEXA

I feel like I read some article about that on NPR's website.

MINNIE

What have I told you about NPR?

LEXA

That it's for pretentious white people or bored housewives.

MINNIE

Stop reading NPR.

Pause.

LEXA (to DRIVER)

Are you a mom?

DRIVER shakes her head.

LEXA

I think I'd be like a trying hard to be cool but really just annoying mom. Like I'd say words like "hip" and "bombtastic" in front of my kid's friends. And I'd let people stay over and then wonder why kid is pregnant at like fifteen.

MINNIE

I have no idea what I'd do with a teen mom. Like what do you even say to that? Use a condom next time?

LEXA

That's not exactly supportive, Minnie.

MINNIE shrugs.

MINNIE

I guess I'd be a shit mom too.

LEXA (to DRIVER)
Do you want kids?

DRIVER takes a while to respond.

DRIVER

I want the idea of children but not actual children.

MINNIE

Yeah. Like there's something cool about having a mini-me but there's something very not cool about having to take care of another human being.

LEXA

I used to want an entire litter of children. Like ten. Remember?

MINNIE

You also used to want to be a marine biologist. Who only worked with seagulls.

A moment.

DRIVER

So. You two are sisters right?

MINNIE nods.

LEXA

Half. We look nothing alike.

MINNIE

We're not even the same race.

LEXA

Race is subjective.

MINNIE shoots LEXA a look.

MINNIE

Our mom was adventurous.

And you're really just taking a cab just to think? Couldn't someone drive you? Sorry if that's too blunt.

LEXA
After everything I've asked you? No. Not all.

MINNIE
Mom couldn't leave work. Quinn had a thing. Lexa's too afraid to tell Seth.

LEXA
I'm not afraid to tell Seth.

MINNIE
Great. Call him right now.

LEXA tenses up.

MINNIE
And I didn't want to take my car across state lines. All of our other friends would be too judgy and Lexa didn't want to fly so...

LEXA
Her tags are expired. (to MINNIE) You're going to get a ticket soon.

MINNIE shrugs. Pause.

LEXA
So no kids but a wife. Did you always know you were gay?

DRIVER
You are the most forward passenger I think I've ever had.

LEXA

It's a long drive. Why not? Let's get heavy.

MINNIE

Could we not get heavy?

LEXA

So what? Just talk about Doctor Who and inventors we want to punch? We're driving to New Mexico so I can abort my unborn child. Who is also the child of my boyfriend. My boyfriend who thinks I'm going to New Mexico to visit my long lost father. What about this situation isn't heavy?

MINNIE

Your dad moved to New Mexico?

LEXA

I don't know where the hell he is. Do you know where Kevin is?

MINNIE

New York.

LEXA

What's in New York?

MINNIE

His loving wife and 28 year old son. Named Mikey.

LEXA

Wait. 28?

MINNIE

Cheated on his wife with mom and then went back. For the baby. And obviously not this one. Get this. Our birthdays are three months apart.

LEXA

How did I not know that?

MINNIE

Because unlike you I keep things to myself.

LEXA

You shouldn't have kept that to yourself.

MINNIE

It's not a thing that just comes up. Hey Lexa I have a half
brother who is the exact same age as me.

LEXA

We don't talk enough. What else are you hiding from me?

Pause.

DRIVER

(attempting to lighten the mood)
My dad's name is Kevin.

MINNIE

(texting) Oh cool. Is he also an alcoholic banker?

DRIVER

No. He's a baseball coach at a high school. Good dad.

MINNIE

Lucky you.

DRIVER

You've got a good mom. Lucky you.

Pause.

30

MINNIE

Speaking of hiding things, you should tell Seth.

LEXA

What?

MINNIE

I mean, not like for permission but just for--you are not a good secret keeper.

LEXA

I am an excellent secret keeper.

MINNIE

You told mom I was gay the second I told you.

LEXA

Not the second.

MINNIE

You texted her while I was telling you.

LEXA

And you're welcome. Mom was super cool about it. You were worried for nothing.

MINNIE

I just feel like this will destroy you if you don't tell him.

LEXA

And say what? And over a text message? "Hey Seth. I'm aborting our unborn child today. No worries. You have no say in it." Yeah that'll go well.

MINNIE

You could call.

LEXA

I could also use a coat hanger.

DRIVER

Jesus.

An awkward and painful silence.

DRIVER

What's Quinn like? That's your girlfriend's name right?

*QUINN comes on stage. She is texting. LEXA
walks over to her.*

MINNIE

She's the best worst person I have ever met.

LEXA

So we should talk.

QUINN

(still texting)
About how you finished your article early and I can finally
put it on the website?

LEXA shakes her head.

MINNIE

She started this online blog thing. As a side job. It's kind of a
mess. But awesome. She writes articles on the news and
current events but they're hilarious. And then she's also got a
blog section called "In my news..." that Lexa curates. Is
curate the right word?

LEXA

(with QUINN) No. It's about...um...it's a little heavy.

QUINN

You think everything is heavy.

LEXA

I'm pregnant.

QUINN stops texting and stares at LEXA.

QUINN

Does Minnie know?

LEXA

You're the first person I'm telling.

QUINN

Shit.

LEXA

Yeah.

QUINN

So not even Se--

LEXA

You are the first person I'm telling. I took five pregnancy tests like three weeks ago and then went to the doctor yesterday. I'm fucking pregnant.

LEXA and QUINN stare at each other.

MINNIE

They don't make a ton of money off the website but the ad revenue and donations are a nice side profit.

QUINN

So. What're--why are you telling me this? Why not your sister or the person who knocked you up?

LEXA
The person who knocked me up?

QUINN
It seems presumptuous to assume

LEXA
It's Seth.

QUINN
Okay. Sorry. I just don't...you seem panicked.

LEXA
I am fucking panicked. I...want to get an abortion.

QUINN
Oh.

LEXA
Oh?

QUINN
Yes. Oh.

LEXA
I'm asking you to drive me and to not tell Minnie. I don't think she could...I don't want mom to know. Or Seth. I just...

QUINN
Lexa, have you really thought this through?

LEXA
Can you take me or not, Quinn?

LEXA and QUINN stare at each other.

MINNIE

Sometimes I think Quinn and Lexa are closer than me and
Lexa. Me and Quinn too. Maybe they should be dating.

LEXA walks away and gets back in the cab.

LEXA

Quinn's not my type. Don't worry Minnie.

DRIVER

Quinn sounds nice.

MINNIE

Half the time she is.

LEXA

It's all really complicated.

MINNIE

I know.

LEXA

You're here for emotional support. Not to lecture me about
Seth.

MINNIE

Okay.

MINNIE stares at the window.

MINNIE

I don't think I ever realized how massive Texas is. Like you
hear it and you study it. But just getting to another state is
like a journey.

LEXA

Yeah. It's prettier though than I thought. All the water in unexpected places.

MINNIE

Traffic and lakes. That should be our state motto.

DRIVER shifts in her seat. LEXA starts to text SETH. She types and erases and types and erases and types

DRIVER

So four years. That's a long time.

MINNIE

It is a long time.

DRIVER

Are you thinking about...

MINNIE

She's not.

LEXA gives up and puts her phone away.

LEXA

I have commitment issues.

DRIVER

Oh.

MINNIE

He's asked. Like twice. Once when they moved from Austin to Houston. And then again on her birthday last year.

DRIVER

And you said no both times?

MINNIE

She said "I have commitment issues."

DRIVER laughs. Who are these people?

DRIVER

Of course.

LEXA

It's complicated.

MINNIE

Obviously. You can't even say I love you over the phone.

LEXA

Not in a text message I don't.

MINNIE

Lexa, you're an I love you whore. I refuse to believe you've never said I love you to Seth.

LEXA

I've never texted it.

DRIVER

I don't text it.

LEXA

It doesn't seem real in a text message. You cannot send a text that's full of emojis one day and then another text with something as heavy as an I love you the next day.

MINNIE

I love you shouldn't be that heavy.

LEXA

Maybe yours aren't. I think it should be sacred. And said
scarcely.

MINNIE

I have legitimately heard you tell Quinn's cat you love her.
Like all the time.

LEXA

I love Pebbles.

MINNIE

You told a tree you loved it.

LEXA

That tree was beautiful.

MINNIE

You're so full of shit.

LEXA

Literally. I'm pregnant.

MINNIE

Geez Lexa.

LEXA

I'm just saying. Neither of you understand what this is like.

MINNIE

You don't even know her.

LEXA

Fine. You, Minerva, do not understand what this is like. You,
driver, you might. I don't know. We're not supposed to be
getting heavy.

MINNIE

She has a name.

LEXA

I don't want to know her name. (to DRIVER) No offense. I don't want to know your name. I don't want--Like if I saw you on the street, I would not say hello.

DRIVER

O-kay.

LEXA

Not because you're a cab driver. I actually think that's really cool. But because of this. This fucked up, awful situation. I want to remember as little about this as I can.

DRIVER

That makes sense.

Pause.

DRIVER

If you're feeling guilty, you don't...

LEXA

It's not guilt. It's...this is one of those times when I would say it's something deep within me. Like in my gut but that just doesn't work because...well there is something in me. That I...It's not guilt.

MINNIE

It's everything else.

LEXA nods. Silence.

DRIVER

John F. Kennedy.

                        LEXA
What?

                        DRIVER
I'd want to punch him in the face.

            LEXA smiles.

                        MINNIE
For Cuba? For the DR?

                        DRIVER
For Marilyn.

            Both MINNIE and LEXA nod.

                        LEXA
What living celebrity would you want to meet like now?

                        MINNIE
Driver? Can we call you driver since we're intentionally not
learning your name?

                        DRIVER
Driver works.

                        LEXA
I feel like that's offensive.

                        MINNIE
You literally told her you wouldn't say hi if you saw her on
the street and you think "Driver" is offensive?

                        DRIVER
I swear. I take no offense. I've been called worse.

MINNIE

Who's your person?

DRIVER

Does she have to be living?

LEXA

I guess not.

MINNIE

Is it Eleanor Roosevelt? Because that's boring.

DRIVER

Mary Shelley.

MINNIE

Like Frankenstein Mary Shelley?

DRIVER

Yeah.

MINNIE

Favorite book?

DRIVER

No. I guess I like the book but her life. What was it like to be the daughter of Mary Wollstonecraft? What were family dinners like?

LEXA
(quoting and having fun with it)
Men and women must be educated by the opinions and matters of the society they live in.

MINNIE

It's manners.

                                LEXA

Really?

                                MINNIE

Yes really.

                                DRIVER

I'm sort of mildly impressed you know who Wollstonecraft
is.

                                MINNIE

For some reason Lexa got me into Women Studies. She
majored. I minored.

                                DRIVER

Huh. Who's your person, Minnie? Phyllis Schlafly?

              DRIVER smiles. MINNIE makes a face in
              response to a text.

                                LEXA

My person, hands down, is Meryl Streep.

                                MINNIE

That's boring.

                                DRIVER

She's kind of a given.

                                LEXA

She is not. I've loved her since Out of Africa. I will love her
forever.

                                MINNIE

This is why I say straight women are boring.

LEXA

Lesbians are boring. Isn't lesbian bed death like a total
thing?

DRIVER

Nope. We cannot--

MINNIE

We're not talking about that.

LEXA

At least straight women are having sex.

MINNIE

Not good sex. Only thirty percent orgasm.

LEXA

It's not thirty

> *LEXA's cut off by her phone ringing. It startles
> MINNIE.*

MINNIE

Fuck.

LEXA

It's Seth.

MINNIE

Pick up.

LEXA

And say what?

MINNIE

Anything.

LEXA picks up the phone.

LEXA

Hey Seth.

MINNIE looks out the window. She sees QUINN. She walks over to her and into the memory.

QUINN

Hey.

MINNIE

Shitty day?

QUINN

Sort of.

LEXA

(in the cab)
Seth, you know Minnie hates it when I'm on the phone.

QUINN

So we don't have secrets right?

MINNIE

Why?

QUINN

I'm trying to figure out the right thing to do.

LEXA

(in the cab)
I don't know. I just thought...I should see my father.

MINNIE

Quinn, you're freaking out. If you've cheated on me or something I don't really care. I mean it's--

44

QUINN

Lexa is having an abortion.

MINNIE shifts.

MINNIE

Okay.

QUINN

Okay?

MINNIE

Okay.

QUINN

She wants me to drive her there.

MINNIE shrugs.

MINNIE

So drive her?

QUINN

I don't exactly agree with it.

MINNIE

Not your place, Quinn.

QUINN

If I'm the driver, it kind of becomes my place doesn't it?

MINNIE

Fine. I'll drive her.

QUINN

You're not supposed to know.

MINNIE

So why are you telling me? To try to stop her?

QUINN

You're her big sister. Maybe you two could go for drinks.

MINNIE

You want me to take my pregnant sister out for drinks but
you don't want her to have an abortion? Since when are you
pro-life?

QUINN

I'm just saying some support for Lexa would be good right
now.

MINNIE

You're her best friend. You really want to support her? Then
drive her to the clinic, hold her hand when she starts
nervously talking about Doctor Who and how guilty she
feels, and cry with her. Don't do this. Whatever the hell this
is.

LEXA

Seriously Seth. I have to go.

MINNIE

I don't know why she told you and not me. And I don't care.
Because it's not about me. Don't make this about you,
Quinn.

> *LEXA hangs up the phone. MINNIE walks back
> over to the cab. LEXA stares out of the window
> at the passing imagery. MINNIE pulls out her
> phone to text.*

                            LEXA

I might re-write it. But, like more seriously.

                            MINNIE

Rewrite what?

                            LEXA

The obituary.

                            MINNIE

Please don't do that to us.

                            LEXA

It's important to me. Maybe when I get back, I can hand it to
Seth and explain it to him that way.

                            MINNIE

You think Seth would understand you had an abortion
because you're handing him an obituary? How does that
make sense?

                            LEXA

I'm tongue tied. I'm a writer. I'm better at reading from a
piece of paper than I am from just emoting.

                            MINNIE

Then write him a letter. Please don't make anyone sit
through another obituary.

                            LEXA

Another? You didn't even let me finish the first one.

                            MINNIE

Because it was terrible. And obviously not what you wrote
down.

LEXA

I couldn't read what I had actually written down. It was too...

DRIVER

Heavy.

LEXA nods.

LEXA

Okay. So here's my deal.

MINNIE

This is sounding too close to another guilt trip.

LEXA

Rape? Fine. You shouldn't be forced to keep a child who is a
constant reminder of tragedy. Incest? Samesies. You could
die? Okay that makes sense. But I'm in a four year
relationship with the person I'm probably going to be with
forever. Like, what's wrong with me? And I haven't even
told him.

MINNIE

Then tell him. Isn't Seth always talking about how much of a
feminist he is?

LEXA

It's not about feminism. It's about...us. And our lives. Like
where do we go from that? Hey Seth. I'm pregnant but I
don't trust you enough to have a family? How does anyone
say something like that?

MINNIE

You just say it. If it's the truth, you have to say it. Or else
you're lying. And that's worse.

LEXA

Some things just shouldn't be said. Look, I'm happy that lesbians can just run around saying everything to each other with no consequence but the rest of us? The consequences outweigh everything else. I can't just pick up the phone and call him. I can't tell him. Ever.

> *TAYLOR comes back on stage. Her energy is different. She's been crying but trying to hide it. DRIVER sees her and walks over but keeps a distance.*

LEXA

Sometimes who you love is way more than important than honesty.

DRIVER

Say something. Please.

TAYLOR

I don't even know how to process this.

DRIVER

It was a mistake.

TAYLOR

A massive, fucked up mistake.

DRIVER

I'm sorry.

TAYLOR

You're always sorry.

LEXA

It's like if you can save your relationship with one lie, why not do it? What good is the truth if it's definite, unchangeable?

TAYLOR

How many times did you sleep with him?

DRIVER shrugs.

DRIVER

I don't know...Three. Maybe.

TAYLOR

Three?

DRIVER

I was drunk. Every time. Black out. Not myself.

TAYLOR

Like so blackout that maybe

DRIVER

No. Taylor. I'm sorry. I was drunk but it was consensual.

TAYLOR

You're a lesbian.

DRIVER

I made a mistake. I'm sorry.

TAYLOR

Fuck.

DRIVER

I know.

TAYLOR

No you don't fucking know.

DRIVER

I--I'm sorry .

TAYLOR

Stop saying sorry.

LEXA

So you just...I don't want him to look at me like that.

MINNIE

Like what?

LEXA

Like I've taken something from him that he'll never get
back. Like I've ripped him.

TAYLOR

And it's over now?

DRIVER

Yes.

TAYLOR

You swear to God?

DRIVER

I swear to God. It's done. It was...

TAYLOR

A mistake.

TAYLOR and DRIVER sit in heavy silence.

LEXA

God, I remember the look Dan gave me when I first told him about Seth. And how I cheated on him. And how I was in love with someone else. I would never stop crying if Seth ever looked at me like that.

TAYLOR

So. He's a partner, isn't he? At the firm?

DRIVER

Yeah.

TAYLOR

Are you going to keep working there?

DRIVER

I can't quit.

TAYLOR

Kate, you're fucking pregnant.

DRIVER

Was.

TAYLOR

Was?

DRIVER

I was pregnant.

Another heavy moment. LEXA shifts.

LEXA

You can see it in their eyes, you know? It's like their pupils start shaking and you know. You know you've just ripped them. They're broken. And they can't ever be fixed.

Pause.

TAYLOR

So you waited to tell me you were pregnant until after you
had an abortion?

DRIVER

I was terrified. And it's not like I wanted to keep it.

*TAYLOR starts to say something. She can't.
Instead*

TAYLOR

I have to go. I can't--I need to leave.

TAYLOR leaves. DRIVER watches her go.

LEXA

I'd cut my own heart out if Seth ever looked at like that.

DRIVER returns to her seat/to driving.

MINNIE

So you'd rather he find out from someone else?

LEXA

He's not going to find out. I only told you and Quinn. I really
only told you because I knew Quinn would tell you.

MINNIE

After you went to the clinic back home. You waited to tell
me after you told Quinn and after you went to the clinic and
after you asked her to pick you up.

LEXA

Okay but seriously. When did Quinn tell you?

MINNIE doesn't say anything.

LEXA
Exactly. You could've talked to me about it.

MINNIE
Most awkward conversation in the world. Hey. You know
that abortion you're planning on having that you didn't want
to talk to me about? Let's talk about it.

LEXA
It's not that I didn't want to talk to you.

MINNIE
Doesn't matter what you wanted. That's how it felt.

LEXA
I didn't want it to be real. I thought the less people I told the
less real it'd be.

MINNIE shifts. Pause.

DRIVER
I get that.

MINNIE
(quietly)
I do too.

*MINNIE stares at the window. Her phone lights
up. She doesn't pay attention to it.*

*LEXA reaches for MINNIE's cigarettes and
lights one. DRIVER hums under her breath.*

Silence. It's a long silence. Suddenly

MINNIE

We'll need gas soon won't we?

DRIVER nods.

MINNIE

Where are we now?

DRIVER

Arlington.

MINNIE

Maybe we should get a drink in Dallas.

Pause.

MINNIE

I'm ready to move.

LEXA

To New Mexico?

MINNIE

No. To, like, Ireland.

LEXA laughs.

LEXA

Driving across Texas that depressing?

MINNIE

No. I just... I want to live on some isle somewhere. Like in a cottage. Grow all my own food. Make my clothes. And like sell the extra for income.

LEXA

That has to be the gayest thing you ever said.

MINNIE

The gayest thing I've ever said was that I like screwing
women.

DRIVER laughs.

LEXA

Is Quinn freaking out?

MINNIE

What do you mean?

LEXA

Like is she...mad?

MINNIE

She drove you to the first clinic.

LEXA

Did she tell you about that?

MINNIE

Not really.

LEXA

She took me to one of those fake clinics.

MINNIE

What?

LEXA

She says she didn't know. And to be fair they do look a lot
like clinics. But yeah it was a crisis pregnancy center.

MINNIE

Are you shitting me?

56

LEXA

I'm sure it was an honest mistake. Those places seem so real.

MINNIE

They are real. They're a real piece of shit.

LEXA

It was a mistake, Min. They're super confusing.

Pause.

MINNIE

She's worried you'll regret it. I doubt it was a mistake.

LEXA

She told me that I'd regret it. But she's not that pushy.

MINNIE

Yes she is.

LEXA

Please don't get in a fight about this. I thought she told you.

MINNIE

That she took you to a fake clinic? No. She told me she took
you a to a very real clinic and that there was some waiting
period or

LEXA

They told me if I had an abortion I'd never be able to have
kids.

MINNIE

They're full of shit, Lexa. Seriously.

LEXA
I know. I thought you'd find it funny.

MINNIE
Too pissed at Quinn.

Beat.

LEXA   (to DRIVER)
So, Quinn. On the ride to the first clinic--well the first place
we went-- the whole time she talked about how Seth and I
would make great parents. Like she didn't ever say don't do
it. She didn't make any speeches about the baby's right to
live. She just kept talking about how awesome Seth and I
would be at parenting. And how sensitive I am.

DRIVER
That's...manipulative.

MINNIE
Yeah. Completely ignoring the fact that Seth is the bad kind
of bipolar working at Starbucks. And you work freelance.

LEXA
It was a mistake, Min.

MINNIE
Sure.

> *MINNIE pulls out her phone. LEXA pulls out her
> Kindle. They all sit in silence.*
>
> *TAYLOR comes back on stage. She's still furious.
> DRIVER walks over.*

DRIVER
Hey.

                              TAYLOR
Hey.

                              DRIVER
I think I'm going to get fired.

                              TAYLOR
Of course.

                              DRIVER
Taylor, I--I realize we're not okay right now but I need you.
I'm going through a really rough time right now and I--I
need my girlfriend right now.

                              TAYLOR
You're an alcoholic.

                              DRIVER
Taylor.

                              TAYLOR
I don't mean that colloquially. I don't mean it in some haha
way. I mean you have a legitimate problem and I don't want
to be with you as it destroys your life.

                              DRIVER
Are you breaking up with me?

                              TAYLOR
You had an abortion without even telling me. You cheated on
me with a man. A man you still work with.

          Pause.

                              DRIVER
I threw up on a client.

TAYLOR doesn't say anything.

DRIVER

Kind of a big client. I mean throwing up on a person is bad enough but this was a client from Big Pharma. You do not throw up on Big Pharma.

TAYLOR still says nothing.

DRIVER

I had a drink before work. Because of all of this was stressing me out.

TAYLOR

All of this?

DRIVER

Us. Fighting. Not being okay.

TAYLOR is silent again.

DRIVER

And I was so stressed out. I just...I thought I'd have one drink and be done with it. But I...I tried to call you but you didn't pick up. And I really, really wasn't okay. So I just

TAYLOR

Got wasted.

DRIVER

I'm going to get fired over this.

TAYLOR is silent.

DRIVER

Talk to me. Please.

TAYLOR

You need to choose. Me or alcohol. If you want to stay with
me, you have to stop drinking. I'm going to sleep at a
friend's house. I'll text you in the morning.

DRIVER

Taylor.

TAYLOR

Don't Kate. If you're sober in the morning we'll figure this
out. If not, I'll move out by the end of the week.

> *TAYLOR leaves. DRIVER lingers. LEXA looks
> up from her Kindle.*

LEXA

I hate when it's quiet.

MINNIE

We know.

> *LEXA reaches for her Kindle. Minnie sends a
> text. DRIVER focuses on the road.*

> *Finally*

LEXA

I just feel like this is when we should get heavy.

> *MOM comes on stage.*

MINNIE

Of course you do.

> *MINNIE puts her phone away.*

DRIVER

You keep saying that but I'm not super sure I understand
what you mean.

LEXA

What's the worst thing that's ever happened to you?

DRIVER

Oh. That's what you mean.

MINNIE

Yeah to Lexa "Let's get heavy" means let's re-live all of our
worst moments and talk about them like we're talking about
how we like our coffee.

LEXA

I just feel like it helps when you're in a crisis to talk about
another crisis you got over. Like to reassure you that this is
something you can get through too.

DRIVER

Well that's a nice way to put it.

LEXA

See. Let's get heavy.

> *A quick beat. MINNIE gets up and walks over to*
> *MOM. MINNIE is not okay.*

MOM

Hey.

MINNIE

Hey.

DRIVER

How dark are we talking?

                           LEXA
How dark are you willing to get?

                           MOM
So, we're not talking about it.

          MINNIE shakes her head.

                          DRIVER
We've still got a decent way to go. I'm not sure we want to
cry for the rest of it.

                           LEXA
Or, maybe we don't cry. Maybe we heal.

          DRIVER gives LEXA a look. Is she serious?

          *MINNIE shifts in her seat. MOM tries to find
          something to say.*

                           MOM
Does your dad still look like a sleazy 70s rock star?

          MINNIE lets out a small smile.

                          MINNIE
He's got short hair now.

                           MOM
Ah. So a sleazy 50s pop star. Is he more Brian Wilson or
Paul McCartney?

          MINNIE smiles.

                          MINNIE
Ringo.

DRIVER
I'm assuming you're also willing to share.

LEXA
I'll go first if everyone else does.

MOM
Figures. So his son's name is Mikey?

MINNIE
Kevin Michael Grant the third.

MOM
Well that's gross.

DRIVER
Losing my job. Almost losing Taylor. That's the worst thing that's ever happened to me.

LEXA
Your job?

DRIVER
Corporate defense. And I was pretty good at it.

LEXA
Oh.

DRIVER
I was also an alcoholic.

LEXA
Oh.

MOM
So what are we going to do?

MINNIE shrugs.

MINNIE
He's my brother, mom. Half but still. My brother.

MOM
He's a son of a bitch. In all the possible ways to mean that.

MINNIE
Mom.

MOM
I'm being serious.

LEXA
Why'd you get fired?

DRIVER
Tons of complicated reasons.

LEXA
Too heavy to talk about?

DRIVER shakes her head.

DRIVER
No. Just...all of it boils down to I was drinking too much and too regularly. I blew a major deal and had a weird relationship with a coworker. They probably should've fired me way sooner.

MOM
As hard as it is we should talk about what happened.

MINNIE
I don't even know how.

MOM nods slowly.

MOM
I'm here for you okay. It's okay. None of this. None of it. Is
your fault.

MINNIE
I kept telling him I was his sister

MOM
I'm so sorry Min.

MINNIE
I screamed no. But no one was home. And I wasn't really
supposed to even be there. I shouldn't have been there. I
shouldn't have gone.

MOM
You're fifteen years old looking for your deadbeat father.
Don't blame yourself.

MINNIE
Mom I--

MINNIE starts to cry. MOM embraces her.

MINNIE
I'm pregnant.

MOM
Jesus.

MINNIE
Yeah. I've never even...I hadn't...

MOM

Oh Minnie. Never?

MINNIE shakes her head.

MINNIE

What am I supposed to do?

MOM

We don't have to have this conversation right now.

MINNIE

No. I want to.

MOM

Are you sure?

MINNIE nods and continues to cry. LEXA leans forward.

LEXA

So the worst thing that's ever happened to me didn't actually happen. I wrote my dad a letter when I was fifteen. Like this long, emotionally letter about how girls need fathers, blah blah blah. And I gave it to my mom to mail it. And she did.

MOM

Honey. You have options. I know it probably doesn't feel like--but you don't have to go through this alone.

MINNIE

What options?

MOM

Well, for one, you don't have to stay pregnant.

LEXA

But what she didn't tell me was that he wrote me back. He mailed it and everything. She opened it and then never gave it to me. I found it like three years ago while I was looking under mom's bed for her money sock.

MINNIE

Mom, I can't...I can't do that. There's no way that I could...

MOM

Okay okay. So adoption?

MINNIE

I don't...I want to...

MOM

If you want to keep it, that's okay too.

MINNIE

No I don't. I...I don't know.

MOM

You don't have to decide right now.

A tense moment.

LEXA

So obviously when I saw it I was infuriated that mom didn't tell me. And then I read it. It said "Real women don't need anything" written on a post-it note and a check for five hundred dollars.

MINNIE

I want...I can't even say the word.

MOM nods.

                              MOM

This is heavy stuff.

                             MINNIE

You sound like Lexa. She's always calling things heavy.

                              LEXA

How could I be mad at mom for hiding that? Like that's the
most confusing thing in the world. My letter was five pages.
FIVE PAGES. And he sends me back a post-it and a check.
If I had seen that at fifteen, that would've destroyed me.

                              MOM

Whatever you decide, Min. Just let me know.

                             MINNIE

Mom?

                              MOM

Yeah Minnie?

                             MINNIE

Please don't tell Lexa about this.

                              MOM

Ever?

                             MINNIE

She's too...I don't think she'd get it.

                MOM nods.

                              MOM

I won't tell her. But you should. Someday.

                *MOM kisses MINNIE on her forehead and then
                leaves the stage.*

MINNIE stares off for a moment and then slowly goes back to the cab. She stares at the window.

Pause.

LEXA

It's your turn.

MINNIE

My turn for what?

LEXA

Minnie you--ugh--What's the worst thing that's ever happened to you?

MINNIE

When I didn't get recruited to that D1 school.

LEXA

Seriously?

MINNIE

I'm not dramatic like you are, Lex. Super tragic things don't happen to me.

DRIVER

What school?

MINNIE

U Penn. For volleyball.

DRIVER

That must've sucked.

MINNIE

It did.

LEXA

She played at UCLA.

MINNIE

It wasn't U Penn.

LEXA

And you totally quit playing. And then you transferred.

MINNIE

I'm not like you. I'm sorry. That was pretty rough for me. I was like eighteen. I thought I was going to go pro.

LEXA

You're absolutely the worst at getting heavy.

MINNIE

Because getting heavy is the absolute worst.

Silence.

DRIVER

What's the best thing?

LEXA

What?

DRIVER

What's the best thing that ever happened to you?

LEXA

That's hard.

MINNIE

Maybe for you, Negative Nancy .

LEXA

Okay. What's the best thing that ever happened to you?

MINNIE

Okay. So we were down like ten points and then--

LEXA

YOU QUIT PLAYING.

MINNIE

It is ridiculously easy to piss you off.

LEXA   (to DRIVER)

So was the best thing that ever happened to you when Taylor and you got married?

DRIVER

It's up there.

MINNIE

But not the best?

DRIVER

The best was the night she decided to stay with me.

LEXA

That's the sweetest thing I've ever heard.

DRIVER

She's by far the best. Now that I think of it meeting her was the absolutely best thing.

> *MINNIE's phone lights up again. MINNIE looks at it and then furiously texts back.*

LEXA

What? Did Quinn forget to change the cat litter?

                            MINNIE
What?

                            LEXA
What's that face you're making?

            Without them seeing it, DRIVER mimics
            MINNIE's face. MINNIE tosses her phone down.

                            MINNIE
Fuck.

                            LEXA
What?

                            MINNIE
Quinn is just...you know she loves you right?

                            LEXA
What did she do?

                            MINNIE
And you know what she's like and how she gets.

                            LEXA
Minnie...

                            MINNIE
And sometimes she just kind of decides what's best for
everyone.

                            LEXA
What happened?

                    Pause.

LEXA

What did she fucking do?

LEXA's phone lights up.

LEXA

It's Seth.

MINNIE

Don't answer.

QUINN comes out on stage pacing.

LEXA

Why not?

MINNIE

Just trust me okay.

*LEXA picks up the phone. MINNIE sees QUINN
and walks over to her.*

LEXA

Seth?

MINNIE

So it didn't go well.

QUINN

Can we talk hypothetically please?

MINNIE

About you very not hypothetically taking my sister to get an
abortion?

QUINN

If we could fix health care and women have maternity leave,
would you still be pro choice?

MINNIE

What the fuck did you say to Lexa?

LEXA

Seth, it's more complicated than that.

QUINN

I didn't say anything. I'm just wondering if I can in good
consciousness continue down this path.

MINNIE

Good consciousness?

LEXA

Seth wait I

QUINN

She's making a mistake.

MINNIE

That doesn't get to be your decision Quinn.

QUINN

I want to offer to take in the baby.

MINNIE

What?

LEXA

Seth no wait.

MINNIE

Have you lost your goddamn mind?

QUINN

We want kids don't we? We could take the baby in. You know we could afford it.

MINNIE

We can?

QUINN

That way the baby stays in the family. Lexa can visit whenever she wants.

MINNIE

No Quinn. Don't do this.

QUINN

I just think it'd be better for everyone involved.

MINNIE

Where's my sister?

QUINN

Minnie.

LEXA

Seth I wanted to tell you. I didn't know how. I didn't want...

MINNIE

Where is Lexa?

> *LEXA looks at the phone. SETH hung up on her. MINNIE gets up and leaves QUINN. MINNIE walks to the cab. QUINN stays on stage.*
>
> *LEXA starts to type something in her phone but MINNIE just hands LEXA her phone.*

MINNIE

I've already got it pulled up.

LEXA

You knew about this?

MINNIE

I just found out, Lex. Around the same time Seth called.

LEXA takes MINNIE's phone.

DRIVER

What's happening?

MINNIE

Quinn published an article on their site. About...this. This whole thing.

LEXA

(reading)
This is how life begins.

QUINN leaves the stage.

MINNIE

She wrote an...I don't know what to call it. I guess an exposé how the US looks at pregnancy and maternity leave and all that shit and basically said...

LEXA

...that if we could fix it we could. Wait. How'd she put it? (reading from the phone) "eradicate the poison that is abortion."

LEXA tosses the phone down.

MINNIE

I didn't even know she was working on it. We had talked
about it.

LEXA

You talked about it?

MINNIE

Not about her writing the article. We just talked about you
and...

LEXA

What about me?

MINNIE

Come on Lexa. You told her first. You had to figure we'd
talk about it.

LEXA

Talk about helping me? Yes. I did. Not talk about how--hold
on let me find it.

LEXA scrolls through the phone.

LEXA

"The desperation of these women has become capital gain."
I'm just a desperate woman, is that it?

MINNIE

You know I don't feel that way. Lexa, seriously. I'm sorry. I
checked the website on a whim. I noticed it and asked Quinn
to take it down. I didn't think she'd show it to Seth.

Pause.

LEXA

She didn't. Technically. Seth saw it too and commented on it.
He said he thought it was just a think piece but then Quinn
told him someone "close to him" was having one.

DRIVER

That's shitty .

LEXA

That's fucking Quinn. I should've...fuck! I should've known
she'd do something like this.

MINNIE

She means well.

LEXA

She probably totally took me to that anti abortion clinic on
purpose.

MINNIE

Yes. That I think she did on purpose.

Pause.

LEXA

I hope she dies.

*LEXA is steaming. MINNIE tries to comfort her
but can't.*

DRIVER

Good news, we're in Wichita Falls. Bad news, I gotta pull
over. We need gas.

MINNIE

Yeah okay. Thanks for letting us know.

The taxi stops and pulls next to a gas station.
LEXA gets out and immediately throws up.
MINNIE gets out and goes into the convenience
store. QUINN walks back out on stage. She
passes MINNIE and goes to LEXA. They run
into each other.

QUINN

I'm just saying you and Seth are a better pair than you think.
Abortion is hard. And I don't think--

LEXA

You know what? Fuck off Quinn. This has nothing to do
with you.

LEXA throws up again. END OF ACT I.

ACT II

> *DRIVER restarts the car. LEXA and MINNIE get back in but are silent. The moment before is still weighing on them.*
>
> *LEXA wipes her mouth and looks out the window. She pulls out her Kindle. MINNIE watches her sister.*
>
> *It's tense. A few more moments before...*

MINNIE

I like the name Alexis.

LEXA

What?

MINNIE

But it's really close to Alexa. Like, ridiculously close. Like why not just name your daughter Alexa?

LEXA

I'm not talking to you.

MINNIE

You're talking to me right now.

LEXA

In, like, general.

> *Silence.*

MINNIE

Like I get the whole gender neutral vibe you were going for. Which is very now so cool. But I just met a guy named Alexis like two weeks ago? And it still took me a minute.

LEXA

Minnie.

MINNIE

Why not Alex? That's a solid gender neutral name. If you'd let me, I'd totally call you Alex.

LEXA

(kind of laughing)
I am not talking to you.

MINNIE

And president? Really Lex? That looks like a shitty job. Like look at pictures of presidents before they go in and then when they come out. They look ragged. And no president can be ever exactly what everyone needs. Half the country will hate your kid no matter what.

DRIVER

And the assassination attempts.

MINNIE

Holy shit. Yes. Not only will half the country hate your kid, every one of those people will try to kill her.

LEXA glares at MINNIE. She wants it to be mean but she is slightly amused.

MINNIE

If it were me, I'd want my kid to go pro.

Pause. MINNIE waits for LEXA to say something. She doesn't.

MINNIE (to DRIVER)

You?

DRIVER

Something classic. Like a lawyer or doctor.

MINNIE

That's boring.

DRIVER

I don't want my kid to have some scandalous life. Boring is nice.

MINNIE

Boring is boring.

Pause.

LEXA

Your girlfriend just told all of our friends, all of our followers, everyone that we know that I was having an abortion.

MINNIE

But I didn't. Why am I being punished for what Cunty Cunterson did?

LEXA laughs despite really not wanting to.

LEXA

You knew.

MINNIE

Not really. My girlfriend bitched about maternity. She didn't say your name once.

                          LEXA
She told Seth.

                          MINNIE
She did do that. Want to call her a cunt so you feel better?

                          LEXA
You know I hate that word. It's beyond the worst thing you
can call a woman.

                          MINNIE
So...fitting?

               *LEXA shakes her head. She's slowly calming
               down.*

                          MINNIE
All of our friends don't know, Lex. They probably think
Quinn is just going on another rant.

                          LEXA
She's trying to guilt trip me.

                          MINNIE
It's Quinn.

                          LEXA
It's shitty.

                          MINNIE
Again. It's Quinn. She's a shitty shitty person. One might
even call her...

                          LEXA
I'm not calling her that.

               LEXA's phone lights up.

84

LEXA

It's Seth.

MINNIE

Throw your phone out the window.

LEXA

That would be a me thing to do.

DRIVER

Want me to roll the window down?

MINNIE nods. DRIVER silently laughs.

MINNIE

Seth could've handled finding out better.

LEXA

He found out from a blog written by my best friend. Worst possible way to find out.

MINNIE

There are worse ways.

LEXA

Minnie.

MINNIE

Well either way he knows now. All your t's have been crossed.

LEXA

You sound like mom.

MINNIE

Well she is my mother.

Pause.

LEXA
Are you going to say anything to Quinn?

QUINN comes out on stage.

MINNIE
(looking at QUINN)
Doubtfully.

LEXA
All of this is her fault.

MINNIE
So maybe not all of it. She didn't get you pregnant.

LEXA
All of it.

MINNIE shrugs and walks over to QUINN.

LEXA deciding to ignore MINNIE pulls out a Kindle and starts reading.

DRIVER tries to say something to LEXA but decides against it.

QUINN
I know you hate me right now.

MINNIE
I don't hate you.

QUINN
You're mad that I want to help Lexa.

MINNIE

I'm mad you want to have a child she doesn't want.

QUINN

She's...she's not like you Minnie.

MINNIE

What?

QUINN

You're not exactly...you would probably handle this situation better.

MINNIE

And why is that Quinn?

QUINN

You don't really have...feelings.

MINNIE

What the fuck Quinn?

QUINN

I'm just saying. Most women regret their abortions.

MINNIE

Actually they don't.

QUINN

Minnie.

MINNIE

Quinn. I am so serious. Do one more shitty thing. Just one. And we're done.

*MINNIE gets up and walks over to the cab. She
pulls out her phone and a portable charger. Still
silence in the cab. MINNIE looks over at LEXA
and what she's reading. She starts to say
something. LEXA's face says don't. TAYLOR
comes on stage. DRIVER notices. DRIVER
walks over to talk to TAYLOR. LEXA keeps
reading. MINNIE starts texting.*

                    TAYLOR
Back from AA?

          DRIVER nods.

                    DRIVER
The meeting was...rough.

                    TAYLOR
Yeah.

          Pause.

                    DRIVER
I want us to be okay.

                    TAYLOR
We're okay.

                    DRIVER
No we're not.

                    TAYLOR
What'd you talk about?

                    DRIVER
At AA?

                    TAYLOR
Yeah.

                    DRIVER
Taylor.

                    TAYLOR
What'd you talk about?

                    DRIVER
You think I didn't go.

                    TAYLOR
I think you didn't go.

                    DRIVER
How long are we going to be like this?

                    TAYLOR
You're an alcoholic and compulsive liar. It was literally your
job.

                    DRIVER
I was not a compulsive liar.

          TAYLOR is silent.

                    DRIVER
You work in finance. You lie just as much as I did.

                    TAYLOR
I don't have a drinking problem.

                    DRIVER
Taylor come on. This isn't living. Do you trust me or not?

TAYLOR

You know I don't trust you.

Pause.

DRIVER

I talked about meeting you in a bar. How so many of my memories. Good and bad happen in bars. Which makes it harder.

TAYLOR relents slightly.

TAYLOR

Be honest with me.

DRIVER

I am.

TAYLOR

You honestly went?

DRIVER nods.

TAYLOR

To the one on sixth?

DRIVER shakes her head.

DRIVER

The one on sixth is on Tuesdays and it's closed. I went to the one twenty eighth. Hell of a walk by the way.

TAYLOR smiles.

TAYLOR

We'll get there.

DRIVER

Back to okay?

TAYLOR nods.

TAYLOR

Just give me some time.

TAYLOR kisses DRIVER on the cheek. They sit together for a moment. DRIVER returns to the car.

A couple seconds of silence but then

MINNIE

I'm just saying I don't want to be punished for Quinn.

TAYLOR leaves the stage.

LEXA

When I get back, I don't think Seth and I will still be together. I don't think he'll forgive me. Not if I go through with it. So it's really hard not to be mad at someone.

MINNIE's phone lights up.

MINNIE

Be mad at Quinn. Be mad at the US. Be mad at Seth for not using a condom. Just not me.

MINNIE checks her phone.

MINNIE

Quinn and I definitely won't be together when I get back. I'd break up with her now but I'd rather just ghost her.

LEXA

How 2016 of you.

MINNIE

I'm very hip.

> *LEXA and DRIVER both react. Quick pause.*
> *Another text to MINNIE's phone.*

MINNIE

(as she's checking her phone)
Quinn. Again.

LEXA

Is she secretly super pro life or something?

> *MINNIE shakes her head.*

MINNIE

No. She's just super pro your specific life.

LEXA

My life.

MINNIE

She thinks you won't be able to handle it.

LEXA

What is there to handle?

> *Pause.*

MINNIE

Okay. New game. What's the worst thing a woman can do
other than get an abortion?

DRIVER

What?

MINNIE

Like in the eyes of the conservative Catholic brand.

LEXA

So basically in the eyes of everyone we grew up around.

MINNIE

Yes.

LEXA

I don't know. Have basic rights?

MINNIE

No. Be serious. What's the worst thing you can think of?

DRIVER

Not including abortion?

MINNIE

Right.

LEXA

Well abortion is murder so murder is out. Because they're equal.

DRIVER

Incest?

MINNIE

Is that really worse than abortion though? Like if someone's dad rapes them, the nuns told us that was an unfortunate blessing.

LEXA laughs.

LEXA

I totally forgot about that. Like, that was word for word how they said it.

MINNIE

I know. (to DRIVER) Did you grow up Catholic?

DRIVER

I didn't. But I know a few people who did.

LEXA

Being gay. But like acting on it. That's worse.

MINNIE

Than abortion?

LEXA

Like full debauchery. Like not only fornicating but all out multiple same sex partners. That's worse.

DRIVER

Is it though?

LEXA

Totally. In the hard core groups, fornication is still a pretty big deal so being gay and fornicating? Please. One way trip to hell.

DRIVER

Are there return tickets?

LEXA

Yes. (to MINNE) Remember all those from hell and back movies gran used to make us watch?

MINNIE

Those were the worst.

DRIVER

That exists?

LEXA

It totally does.

Pause.

MINNIE

I'm sorry about Quinn.

LEXA

It's okay. I mean, it's so not okay. But you're right. You
didn't do it.

MINNIE

I should've told you earlier. That we'd been arguing about it.
I was pressuring you to tell Seth because I knew it was only
a matter of time before she did.

LEXA nods.

LEXA (to DRIVER)

What's Taylor doing tonight?

*TAYLOR comes out on stage with a book and is
reading.*

DRIVER

Probably reading.

MINNIE

What kind of books does she like?

DRIVER

The ones with words in them.

LEXA and MINNIE smile.

MINNIE

Lexa's like that. She'll read anything in front of her.

LEXA

There is nothing wrong with literacy.

DRIVER gets up and walks over to TAYLOR.

DRIVER

I love you.

TAYLOR

I know.

DRIVER

Why'd you stay? Even after...

TAYLOR

After you cheated on me, had an abortion, relapsed, lied about your alcoholism...

DRIVER

All of it. I was awful.

TAYLOR

I stayed because I love you too.

Pause.

DRIVER

I love y --

TAYLOR

But more than that. I believe in you.

DRIVER smiles.

DRIVER

Two things. I got a job today.

TAYLOR

As what? A janitor?

DRIVER

Taxi driver. I start tomorrow.

> *A moment of silence. MINNIE's and LEXA's phone lights up. TAYLOR kisses DRIVER on the cheek.*

TAYLOR

Are you okay with that?

DRIVER

What? Going from being one of the best lawyers to being a taxi driver?

TAYLOR

It sounds so judgmental when you put it like that.

DRIVER

I think it's a great way to start over. Plus I like driving. Always have.

TAYLOR

You do. Such a weirdo. The only person I know who doesn't curse in traffic.

DRIVER

I like driving. Even when I'm not actually moving. There's just something...I don't know equally safe and dangerous about being in a car. I also like people.

TAYLOR

Most people.

Pause.

TAYLOR

What's the other thing?

DRIVER

Oh that.

DRIVER reaches into her pocket and takes out a ring. TAYLOR looks at it smiling.

DRIVER

I thought about asking in some grandiose way but...

TAYLOR

Oh.

DRIVER

Yeah. I realize you have no reason to say yes right now. And that is beyond fair. But this is me asking.

TAYLOR

No one knee?

DRIVER

Not yet. I realize I have a lot to make up for but when you're ready to marry me let me know by putting on that ring. Absolutely whenever you are ready. And we'll get married that day.

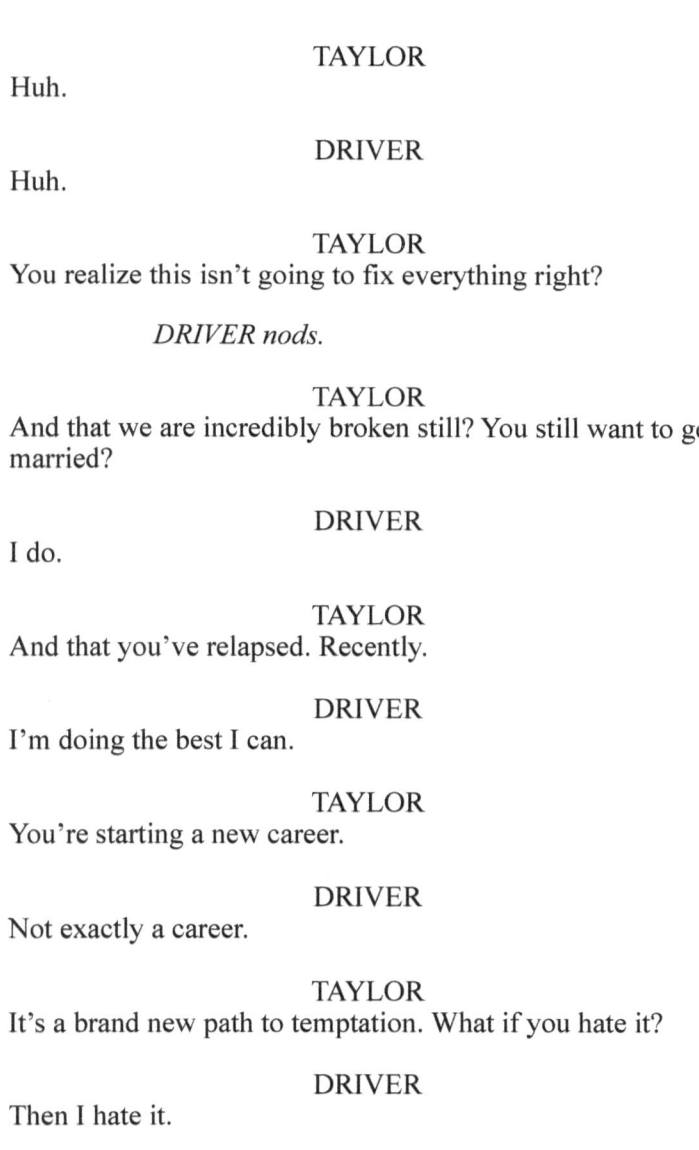

TAYLOR

Huh.

DRIVER

Huh.

TAYLOR

You realize this isn't going to fix everything right?

DRIVER nods.

TAYLOR

And that we are incredibly broken still? You still want to get married?

DRIVER

I do.

TAYLOR

And that you've relapsed. Recently.

DRIVER

I'm doing the best I can.

TAYLOR

You're starting a new career.

DRIVER

Not exactly a career.

TAYLOR

It's a brand new path to temptation. What if you hate it?

DRIVER

Then I hate it.

> *Pause. TAYLOR reaches for the ring and puts it on.*

DRIVER

Really?

TAYLOR

Really. I mean, if this blows up in our faces, divorce is still a thing right?

> *DRIVER goes over and kisses TAYLOR. TAYLOR checks the time.*

TAYLOR

It's a bit late. We might have to wait to get married tomorrow.

DRIVER

I love you.

TAYLOR

I know.

> *DRIVER kisses TAYLOR again and then goes back into the cab. TAYLOR lingers for a bit staring at the ring before leaving.*

> *MINNIE looks at her phone and then out the window. LEXA leans forward.*

> *Pause.*

LEXA   (to MINNIE)

You're looking terrible. What happened?

MINNIE

Guess.

                    LEXA

Quinn?

                    MINNIE

Seth is there. Crying.

                    LEXA

There?

                    MINNIE

Our apartment.

                    LEXA

Why would he go to Quinn?

                    MINNIE

Where the hell else was he going to go?

                    LEXA

His own friends. Any of them.

                    MINNIE

And then cry about his girlfriend's pending abortion?

                    LEXA

Fair enough. (pause) New game.

                    MINNIE

Seriously?

                    LEXA

What am I supposed to do about Seth crying? Turn the cab
around?

                    DRIVER

I don't mind if that's what--

LEXA

No. That's not happening. It can't happen. This has to happen now.

DRIVER

Okay.

MINNIE

But why though? You're still early on and...

LEXA

Seriously? Are you okay with this or not?

Pause.

MINNIE

I get really exhausted by how many people expect me to want children.

LEXA

I don't...what just happened?

MINNIE

I was just thinking about it. Like if you don't want kids and you're a woman, you're a terrible human being. You get to a certain age and it's like everything else fails to matter. Like, Driver, how often do people ask if you have kids?

DRIVER

All the time.

MINNIE

You're a woman of a certain age and all anyone wants to talk about

                    DRIVER
Kids.

                    MINNIE
Exactly.

                    LEXA
Is this you trying to convince me to turn the cab around?

                    MINNIE
This is me, pulling a you.

            LEXA smiles.

                    LEXA
(smiling)
Let's get heavy.

                    MINNIE
Like seriously? Am I worthless because I don't want
children?

                    LEXA
(kidding)
Yes. Women are supposed to have kids. It is our evolutionary
duty to procreate.

                    MINNIE
I was talking to this woman on the bus once and I was just
saying I was tired. That was it. And then she goes "You don't
know tired. Wait until you have kids. Then you'll know
tired." Seriously? Do moms own emotions now?

                    LEXA
Yes.

MINNIE and DRIVER laugh.

DRIVER

My mom told me the other day "Just because you're
choosing this life, that doesn't mean children aren't an
option."

MINNIE

Geez.

DRIVER

Exactly.

MINNIE

And like no mom I have ever talked to seems to actually like
it. Like it's always the whole my kids ruined my dreams,
ruined my business, ruined my life but oh. Of course I still
love them. With that like half smile. That no one, ever,
anywhere, believes.

LEXA

That's not fair. I think a woman can have kids and love kids
and still feel...sad for the life they didn't have. It's not their
fault society--

MINNIE

Lexa

LEXA

Not the right moment?

> *MINNIE and DRIVER both shake their heads.*
> *Pause.*

MINNIE

If you don't want a kid, don't fucking have one. But call
your crying boyfriend. Tell him the truth. Have a
conversation and if it ends in a break up then okay.

But don't throw it all away. Because you won't regret the
abortion. But you'll regret losing him. And I don't want that
for you.

LEXA shakes her head.

LEXA

I can't. I'm not..

MINNIE

Okay.

Pause.

LEXA

Who?

MINNIE

What?

LEXA   (to DRIVER)

No. Who? Who do you know who had an abortion? I know
you didn't answer but I just assumed

MINNIE

Lexa.

LEXA

You don't have to answer. I just...if it was someone close to
you, did they...do they talk about it?

MINNIE

You can't ask things like that.

DRIVER

It was me. I did.

LEXA

Oh. Oh. I'm sorry for all the murder talk earlier. I was just...

DRIVER

It's fine. I got it.

LEXA

What...happened? Is that too heavy?

DRIVER

It's not heavy. Just not exactly something I want to think
about.

LEXA

Do you regret it?

DRIVER shakes her head.

DRIVER

I regret how I got pregnant but the abortion? No. Not even a
little bit.

LEXA

But how'd you know you'd be okay?

DRIVER

I trusted myself. It didn't really feel like any of the other
options were right.

LEXA

So it wasn't...the father wasn't someone you loved?

DRIVER

It was someone I didn't even like.

Pause.

LEXA

I've ruined Seth.

MINNIE

This isn't about Seth. What do you want Lexa? If you want we can just go home and talk about all of this tomorrow?

LEXA

And waste $1200? Are you kidding? We have to pay her.

DRIVER

Listen. Just...it's okay. We still haven't even made it to the border. I can turn around. And I can keep five hundred

LEXA

No. I don't...I don't want to turn around. I want to keep going. I have to keep going. I know that I want to do this.

MINNIE

You're sure?

LEXA

Yes. I don't want to be pregnant.

DRIVER

Okay.

LEXA

I'm just...I know this is something that needs to happen. I hate all of the collateral.

MOM steps out with two glasses of wine.
MINNIE gets out of the cab and walks over to
MOM. MOM hands her a wine glass.

DRIVER

The collateral is the worst part. But it'll get better. Especially if you're honest. Or at least it did for me.

MINNIE stares suspiciously at the glass.

MOM

What? Are you going to tell me you don't drink? I've seen your friends, Minnie.

MINNIE

I don't drink wine.

MOM

Sure Minnie. Will you at least try it?

MINNIE tries the wine. She doesn't like it.

MINNIE

What's this for?

MOM

It's been a year. Today.

MINNIE

Mom.

MOM

You were sulking this morning. Lexa saw you.

MINNIE

Where is Lexa?

                    MOM

Honors something.

                    MINNIE

You haven't told her right?

                    MOM

I promised you I wouldn't. But someday

                    MINNIE

I know I know. At some point I should tell Lexa. What's the
wine for? It's like noon.

                    MOM

We're celebrating.

                    MINNIE

We're celebrating the worst day of my life?

            *MOM finishes her wine and embraces her
            daughter in a subtle but loving way.*

                    MOM

We are celebrating the day you took your body back.

            MINNIE finishes off her wine.

                    MINNIE

It still doesn't feel like mine. And I hate...I thought I'd wake
up and be fine. But I'm not. I'm not okay.

            MOM kisses MINNIE on the forehead.

                    MOM

Then we'll drink, every year, on this day. And hopefully one
of those days, in one of those years, it will feel like yours
again.

MOM leaves the stage. MINNIE drinks the wine, takes a moment, and then returns to her seat.

LEXA reaches for her phone but doesn't dial.

LEXA

Do you think protestors will be there?

MINNIA and DRIVER share a look.

MINNIE

Yea, Lex. I think so.

LEXA

Are they not the worst?

LEXA sinks into the seat. She's not crying but she's also not okay. Pause.

MINNIE

Quinn moved out for a week after I told her about my abortion.

LEXA glares at MINNIE. MINNIE lights another cigarette. QUINN comes out on stage.

LEXA AND QUINN

I'm sorry. Your what?

MINNIE doesn't say anything.

LEXA

How did I not know this?

QUINN

Why didn't you tell me?

MINNIE

Yeah. I told her after she took you and she started talking
about taking in the kid and--

LEXA AND QUINN

You had an abortion?

MINNIE

It was a while ago. And it doesn't really matter. The point
is--

QUINN

Of course it matters.

LEXA

Minnie. I--what?

MINNIE

It happened in high school. Mom and I had our own abortion
road trip.

LEXA

Mom knows?

QUINN

This is like a massive thing to hide from someone. This
is...this is a betrayal.

MINNIE

Quinn totally flipped out. I had no idea why. I said it in
passing. And she just lost her shit.

QUINN

I gotta get out of here. I just...you're seriously not going to
tell me what happened?

LEXA

Was it some guy in high school? Weren't you sleeping
with..Was it Jefferson? He's the only person you slept with
in high school. I knew that bastard was not to be trusted.
Who sleeps with their student? Oh. Is that why you want to
punch him?

MINNIE doesn't say anything. QUINN exits.

MINNIE

It was a fucking disaster. That's all that matters.

LEXA

Did he...was it...Minnie. Did he rape you?

MINNIE

It wasn't Jefferson. Random guy. And it wasn't...it wasn't
like this exact situation.

LEXA

Minnie. Holy shit. You cannot tell me in a cab that you had
an abortion and that you were raped. I mean...holy shit.
That's not the kind of thing that you--

MINNIE

It doesn't matter, Lexa. What matters is that moment doesn't
make me the worst. It makes me a girl

LEXA

Young woman who was raped

MINNIE

Stop saying rape. I was a girl who was in a situation

DRIVER

A shitty situation

MINNIE

And I found a way out.

Silence.

LEXA

I didn't want it to get that heavy.

MINNIE smiles.

MINNIE

All I'm trying to say is not everybody has the same way out.

LEXA nods. And then laughs. Suddenly.

LEXA

Did mom call it the abortion road trip?

MINNIE

She totally did.

DRIVER

Such a cool mom.

LEXA and MINNIE both visually agree.

LEXA

But cool dad, right?

DRIVER

Cool dad.

LEXA

On a scale of one to ten how mad would you be if I finished my obituary?

MINNIE

You would really do that to us? I just told you my deep dark secret.

LEXA

I feel like a good obituary should be funny.

DRIVER

I have literally never laughed at an obituary.

LEXA

And have you ever read one and went "Whoa cool obituary."

DRIVER

I have not.

> *LEXA reaches for her phone to write the obituary.*

LEXA

Oh. Seth called again.

> *She opens up notes in her phone.*

LEXA

Okay. So where do we start?

MINNIE

Can we start by calling Seth?

> *LEXA over dramatically pouts.*

DRIVER

I think it's pretty fair to say Alex is a better gender neutral name than Alexis.

LEXA

What about River?

MINNIE

River Pearson? Sounds like a place not a person.

LEXA

But it's like super hippie.

MINNIE

Which you are not.

DRIVER

You have a kindle.

LEXA

And that makes me not a hippie?

MINNIE

You are constantly touching your phone. Aren't hippies all
about conserving energy?

LEXA

The boring ones.

DRIVER

You mean the real ones?

LEXA

Okay, okay. Moon.

MINNIE

Now you're just fucking around.

LEXA

I am. I'm sticking with River who I think we should have
like an effigy for.

                              DRIVER
Are you sure that's--

                              MINNIE
Define effigy.

                              LEXA
What?

                              MINNIE
I don't think that word means what you think it does.

                              LEXA
It's when you like light incense and throw a bunch of stuff
into a fire and then say a nice prayer after to--

                              MINNIE
It's a statue.

                              LEXA
Really?

                              DRIVER
Really.

                              LEXA
Oh hell no. I don't want that.

            MINNIE and DRIVER both smile.

                              MINNIE
So River?

            LEXA's phone lights up again. It's SETH.

                         LEXA

I can't.

                        MINNIE

Then don't.

                         LEXA

I will.

                        MINNIE

I know.

            MINNIE pulls out her phone.

                        MINNIE

Fuck.

                         LEXA

What?

           MINNIE shows LEXA her phone.

                         LEXA

Jesus.

                        DRIVER

Quinn?

                         LEXA
She posted a picture of Seth crying to her blog post.

                        DRIVER

Well that's exciting.

                        MINNIE
I think it's pretty fair to say I had no idea she was going to
do that.

LEXA

You gotta give it to her. She's really standing up for what she believes in.

MINNIE

Yeah. By being a sociopath.

LEXA

She's your special sociopath.

MINNIE's phone lights up. It's QUINN.

LEXA

You should talk to her.

MINNIE

I'm not really in the mood to talk to Satan right now.

DRIVER laughs.

DRIVER

Will Seth be okay?

LEXA nods and pulls out her phone.

LEXA

I am texting him to tell him I'll call him when I get to New Mexico.

MINNIE

I can't believe Quinn put a picture of him crying online.

LEXA

Our friends definitely know now.

DRIVER

Satan.

MINNIE

Exactly.

Pause.

LEXA

I'm not over you never telling me about your abortion.

MINNIE

I know.

LEXA

Like that's massive.

MINNIE

Like telling my girlfriend about your abortion before telling me massive?

LEXA

You mean the girlfriend who just posted a picture of my crying boyfriend online? I'm going to win this one, Min.

The car makes a strange noise. LEXA and MINNIE turn to DRIVER.

DRIVER

I gotta pull over.

LEXA

What's wrong with the car?

DRIVER

Coolant. I have to refill it.

MINNIE

We could use a break anyway.

> *DRIVER pulls over. They all get out of the car.*
> *DRIVER grabs the coolant.*

MINNIE

Wait a minute.

DRIVER

To put coolant in?

MINNIE

Doesn't the engine have to cool down anyway?

> *DRIVER shrugs.*

DRIVER

I guess so.

> *DRIVER, MINNIE, and LEXA sit on the curb.*
> *MINNIE reaches into her bag and pulls out a*
> *cheap bottle of red wine.*

LEXA

What is that?

MINNIE

It's wine.

LEXA

I can see that.

> *MINNIE screws off the top.*

MINNIE

You're right. I should've told you about my abortion. I should've told you years ago.

LEXA

Yes you should have.

MINNIE

But remember when you said the less people you told the less it felt real?

LEXA nods. And then gets it.

LEXA

Still though.

MINNIE

I know.

MINNIE's phone lights up. She ignores it.

MINNIE

I didn't know how to talk about it with anyone, Lex. I made mom swear not to tell you anyone.

LEXA

That was probably really hard for her.

MINNIE

Probably. I'm sorry, okay? I don't like to "get heavy." It hurts too much. Some things I'd like to never ever have to talk about again.

LEXA

Yeah.

DRIVER

Why the wine?

MINNIE

I'm happy you asked. When I was just...fucked up over everything mom made me drink terrible wine.

LEXA

She made you?

MINNIE nods.

MINNIE

And it was gross.

DRIVER

Was it gas station wine?

MINNIE

Knowing mom

MINNIE takes a big gulp.

MINNIE

She told me we'd drink every year on the same day I got my abortion until my body felt like mine again. So, here.

MINNIE hands LEXA the bottle.

LEXA

Is today that day?

MINNIE

No. But today is your day. So here we are. In the Texas...wait.

MINNIE looks further down the road.

                              MINNIE
We're at the fucking border.

                              DRIVER
About a few feet off but yeah.

                              MINNIE
Get it, Lex. We're crossing the border.

            LEXA smiles and drinks the wine. It's disgusting.

                              LEXA
Jesus.

                              MINNIE
Yeah it's pretty bad.

            LEXA tries to pass the bottle to DRIVER.

                              DRIVER
AA remember?

                              LEXA
Shit sorry.

                              MINNIE
Wait.

                  *MINNIE reaches in her bag and pulls out grape
                  juice.*

                              MINNIE
I didn't forget about you.

                  *MINNIE tosses the bottle to DRIVER. DRIVER
                  smiles.*

DRIVER

Was this the most disgusting grape juice you could find?

MINNIE

Yes. Juice is nowhere on the bottle. It's grape drink.

DRIVER nods and drinks it.

DRIVER

Oh that it is not...

LEXA

Yeah that's how we feel.

DRIVER

So why I am also drinking with you?

MINNIE

You told two strangers you had an abortion and you can't even drink about it. Sucks.

DRIVER smiles.

DRIVER

You two aren't so bad.

> *A moment. It's a sweet moment. LEXA pulls out her phone.*

LEXA

(talkings as she types in her phone) River Falcon Pearson was the envy of all her friends.

MINNIE

You're seriously going to make us sit through another obituary?

DRIVER
After graduation from Yale, River graduated summa cum laude

MINNIE
No. Not you too.

LEXA
From Yale she went on to join Peace Corps.

MINNIE
That's pretentious.

LEXA
Her name is River. She'd probably be pretentious.

DRIVER
She lived in Honduras and met the love of her life.

LEXA
Then she returned to the United States with her love to

LEXA looks at MINNIE.

MINNIE
No. I will not participate in this. This is super unhealthy.

DRIVER
To fight for migrant rights.

LEXA
Yes!

DRIVER and LEXA cheer their glass/juice.

MINNIE

You're both insane.

LEXA continues typing. MINNIE pulls out a
cigarette. DRIVER finishes her juice and then
grabs the coolant. DRIVER puts the coolant in
the car.
She motions to the car.

DRIVER

You ready?

MINNIE and LEXA look at each other.

LEXA

Yeah. I think I am.

LEXA finishes the wine and gets in the cab.
MINNIE puts her cigarette out and gets back
into the cab.

DRIVER starts the cab up again.

MINNIE

You drank all that wine? You're totally going to have to pee
soon.

LEXA

I already have to pee.

MINNIE nods and reaches for her headphones.
LEXA taps on MINNIE's shoulder before
MINNIE puts the headphones in.

LEXA

You're my actual favorite.

MINNIE

You da best.

> *LEXA smiles as MINNIE puts her headphones in. LEXA pulls out her kindle. DRIVER turns on the radio. They're okay. All of them. END of play.*